MW01181232

Part of a Comprehensive Multicultural Program
Kindergarten/Elementary Level

AUTHOR

C. Alta received her bachelor's degree in Early
Childhood Education from Purdue University. An author
of other children's books and a mother of two, she is
involved in educating children about love and life
through her tender thoughts and words.

ILLUSTRATOR

Ray Hecita graduated from The Art Institute of
Seattle and is currently an editorial illustrator.
He illustrates in a way that captures the
imagination of young minds.

DESIGNER

Kimberly Shaw

PROJECT EDITOR

Rizwan Awan

PROJECT CONSULTANTS

M. "Minhaj" Khokhar
Rafiah Al-Ansari

Amica International
1201 First Avenue South
Suite 203
Seattle, WA 98134
(206) 467-1035
Fax: (206) 467-1522
Outside Seattle: 1-800-622-9256

ISBN# 1-884187-04-8
Library of Congress Card Number: 94-071172

GOD CREATED EVERYTHING

Written by
C. Alta

Illustrated by
Ray Hecita

PEOPLE
of the
WORLD
series ™

People of the world series is a trademark of Amica Publishing House
distributed and marketed by Amica International

The Blades of Grass

The Oceans and Seas
The Rocks

The Soil
The Beautiful Trees
The Majestic Mountains
That We See

God Created Everything

The Dog
The Cow

The Whales
The Birds, The Spider, and Bees

The Wild

The Tame

God Created Everything

The Sun

The Moon

The Rainbow
The Clouds
Tornados, Volcanos
Lightning Shattering the Skies

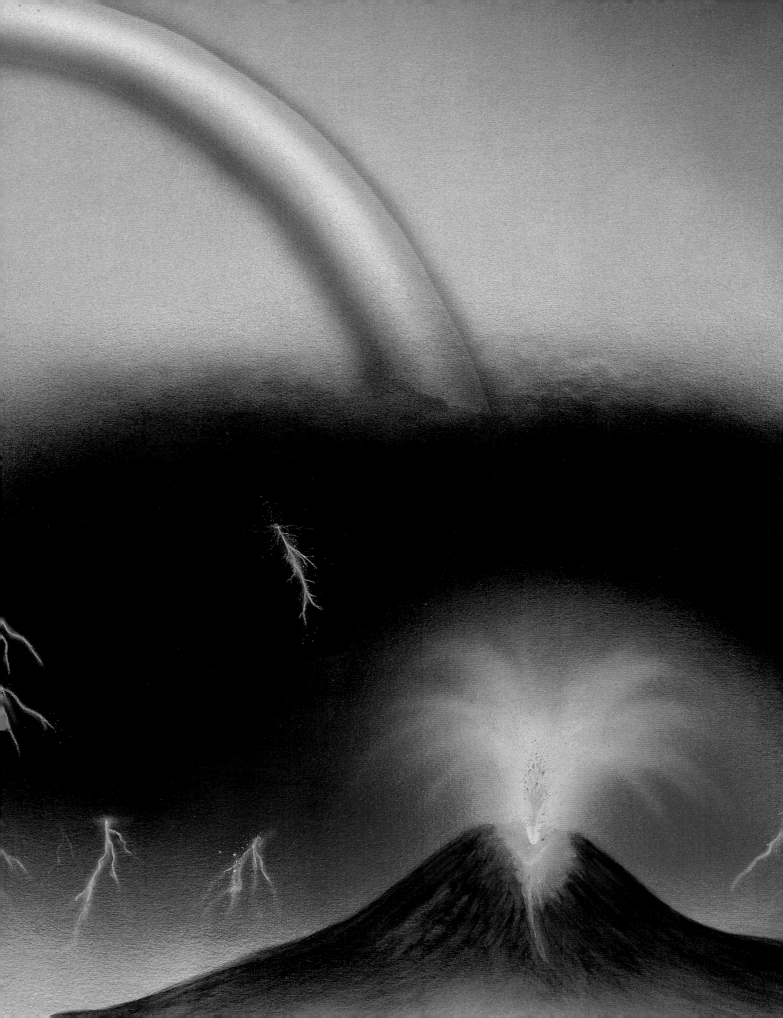

People Of The World
Shapes
And Colors We See

God Created Them
Just Like You And Me

GOD CREATED EVERYTHING

Written by

C. Alta

The Blades Of Grass,
The Oceans And Seas,
The Rocks -
The Soil -
The Beautiful Trees,
The Majestic Mountains That We See,
God Created Everything.

The Dog -
The Cow -
The Whales -
The Birds, The Spiders And Bees,
The Wild -
The Tame -
God Created Everything.

———➤•◆•◄———

The Sun,
The Moon,
The Rainbow -
The Clouds -
Tornadoes, Volcanos,
Lightning Shattering The Skies.

People Of The World,
Shapes -
And Colors We See,
God Created Them
Just Like You And Me.